Christmas Programs for the Church

Compiled by
Brynn Robertson

Standard® PUBLISHING
Bringing The Word to Life

Cincinnati, Ohio

Standard Publishing
Cincinnati, Ohio.
A division of Standex International Corporation
© 2006 by Standard Publishing

ISBN 0-7847-1648-X

Contents

The Perfect Gift

by Tekoa Miller

Summary: A poetic look into the struggle of a boy with no money to find the perfect Christmas gift for his mother.
Character:
BOY—a teenage boy
Costume: raggedy winter clothing including coat and hat

BOY: The snowflakes fell on that cold winter day. A little boy hurried by, shivering in the gray. He suddenly stopped; a shop window caught his eye. It was hidden in the corner, not visible to a passerby. A beautiful music box, shimmering with gold. With that in his sight, the boy forgot about the cold. It was the perfect gift; his mother would smile. His face fell. That was something he hadn't seen in a while. He gazed at the box with its glimmering case and a determined look came over his face. The boy stopped off at the very next shop. "Do you need some help to clean and mop?" The owner looked at him and finally agreed. So the boy grabbed a mop and set to work with great speed. When he finished, the shopkeeper gave him a dime. The boy thanked him and hurried to see what other jobs he could find. All down the street, he went into each store and at each stop, he asked if they needed help with some chores. At the end of the day, his muscles felt dead but he smiled with satisfaction as he climbed into bed. The very next day, he set out like before because he was determined to knock on every single door. From washing dishes to taking out the trash he helped each person complete their daily tasks. That night before he drifted off to sleep, he piled all his coins in a small heap. He counted his money again to make sure he was right. He could hardly wait to see the beautiful sight. Early the next morning, he dressed fast as he could. He buttoned up his coat and pulled up his hood. He was out of breath by the time he reached the store. He was so early, they hadn't yet opened the door. The boy peered through the window—yes, there it lay. He could almost hear what his mother would say. The boy smiled proudly, "She'll love it, I'm sure. I've found the perfect gift for her." He reached into his pocket to finger the money for his prize. The boy's face turned white.

"It's gone," he realized. He felt again, but to his dismay, there was nothing but a hole where his money once laid. Quickly, he turned and retraced his steps. He searched for hours on end until he was cold and wet. Defeated, he turned for home with a sigh. He sat down on his bed and began to cry. It was far too late to earn more money now. He wanted the perfect gift for his mom, but how? He had no choice. He had to give in. The boy never wanted to see Christmas like this again. Christmas morning came with a beautiful blanket of snow but the little boy didn't look at the wintry show. He didn't even notice the glorious tree. He turned to his mom and said, "I'm so sorry. I tried to find a present to make you smile. I did my best, but I failed all the while." His mom sat beside him and held him close. She said, "There's something you must know. To celebrate Jesus, we give gifts to each other but that sentiment has been lost to another. During the holidays, people become consumed with greed. My son, you're the only Christmas present I need." I should probably tell you that little boy was me. I went to bed that night happier than I thought I could be.

[Blackout.]

Christmas Idol

by John Cosper

Summary: A reality show gives three judges a chance to pick who is the ultimate Christmas idol.

Characters:

RYAN—the incredibly cheesy host of the show, should be a young man

ANDY—a middle-aged man who thinks he is a rapper, contest judge

DARLA—a middle-aged woman who is nice to everyone but doesn't like SILAS, contest judge

SILAS—a middle-aged man with an English accent, thinks very highly of himself, rude to most people, contest judge

FROSTY THE SNOWMAN

RUDOLPH

SANTA

SCROOGE

THE THREE KINGS—three men, nonspeaking roles

Setting: TV studio

Props: table, microphone, bright orange hunting cap

Costumes: modern-day clothing including a sparkly and obnoxious shirt for DARLA, tight black T-shirt for SILAS, and oversized button-down shirt for ANDY, suit for RYAN, reindeer costume, SANTA costume, suit for SCROOGE, FROSTY THE SNOWMAN costume, Bible-times costumes for the THREE KINGS

Theme music plays. Lights up. RYAN is at center. The judges are seated at a table stage right.

RYAN: Welcome back to *Christmas Idol*. I'm Ryan Cheesefest. This holiday season, our judges went around the world looking for the individual that most represents the holiday season.

[FROSTY enters.]

FROSTY: Hi, I'm Frosty the Snowman. I'm so Christmassy, I'm made out of snow! I've got a corncob pipe, a button nose, and I'm just the jolliest guy you'd ever meet.

RYAN: Well, you sure look jolly. Judges, what do you say?

DARLA: Aw, Frosty, you're so cute. You're the perfect winter weather friend.

ANDY: Yo, yo, dog, check this out. I've never seen someone like you. You're full of snow. This is true.

RYAN: And how about you, Silas?

SILAS: Frosty? Bah, humbug!

DARLA: Oh come on, Silas! He's so cute, and he's made of snow. Plus, his fashion is excellent. That scarf and hat combination is incredible!

SILAS: Am I the only one who remembers that it's Christmas in the south too? He'd melt away on Miami Beach. He's a pathetic excuse for a Christmas idol. Get out of here!

[FROSTY frowns and exits.]

RYAN: Sorry, Frosty. Better luck next time. Who is our next contestant? He's furry! He's friendly!

[RUDOLPH enters].

RUDOLPH: Hi there, folks! I'm Rudolph the red-nosed reindeer and I love Christmas! I love it so much that when I think of it, my nose lights up all red and bright!

DARLA: Aww, Rudolph, that's so cute! I love it. And red *is* in this season!

RUDOLPH: Thanks, Darla. I think you're cute too!

ANDY: Yo, yo, yo, dog!

RUDOLPH: I'm not a dog. I'm a reindeer.

ANDY: Yo, you call yourself a reindeer? I call you full of Christmas cheer.

RYAN: How about it, Silas?

SILAS: Are you daft? You know, the problem here is the holiday season coincides with hunting season. We send him out, he's liable to get shot.

DARLA: Who would shoot a sweet deer like him?

SILAS: *[puts on a hunting cap]* Me, for one. Nothing like venison for Christmas dinner.

[RUDOLPH screams and runs offstage.]

DARLA: I can't believe you're such a jerk! Eating deer?

SILAS: What do you think I brought to last year's potluck dinner?

DARLA: You said it was pheasant!!!

RYAN: OK, folks, let's move right along. Our next contestant hails from the North Pole.

[SANTA enters.]

SANTA: Ho, ho, ho! Merry Christmas!!

DARLA: Santa! It's Santa!!

ANDY: Ho, ho, ho and hee, hee, hee, Santa, yo, he's da man for me!

RYAN: Sounds like we have a winner. Silas?

SILAS: Let's see. He's old. He frightens small children. Is that what we are looking for?

DARLA: Silas! I can't believe you're saying this about Santa.

SILAS: I can't believe no one's said it before!

ANDY: Silas, you the lowest thug! Why you gotta say humbug?

SILAS: I only speak the truth. Santa, hit the gym!

SANTA: Looks like someone wants to be on the naughty list again!

SILAS: Oh wow, I'm shaking in my stockings. Get lost.

[SANTA exits.]

DARLA: Jerk.

RYAN: Let's see if our next contestant can fare any better. Welcome from jolly old England, Ebenezer Scrooge.

[SCROOGE enters.]

RYAN: Merry Christmas, Mr. Scrooge.

SCROOGE: Christmas? Bah humbug!

DARLA: Whoa! That's the last thing we need is an old humbug! Andy?

ANDY: Yo' dog, I'd rather do the luge than vote for Ebenezer Scrooge.

RYAN: Silas, what do you say?

SILAS: Are you kidding? He's the perfect symbol for Christmas!

DARLA: Oh my goodness!

SILAS: I'm serious! Who isn't tired of the commercialism of Christmas? All those stupid TV specials? And that kid with the BB gun 24 hours straight?

DARLA: That's it! I'll be in my trailer!

[DARLA stands and exits.]

ANDY: Peace on earth and peace out!

[ANDY exits.]

SILAS: You're only mad because I'm right!

[SCROOGE exits. THE THREE KINGS enter.]

RYAN: We'll be back to find out what Silas has to say about these guys from the East?

[Theme music plays. Blackout.]

Questions of the Innkeeper's Wife

by Diana C. Derringer

Summary: If the innkeeper, who provided a place for Mary and Joseph on the night Jesus was born, were married, his wife probably had several questions about the event.

Character:

THE INNKEEPER'S WIFE—middle-aged woman **Props**: an old style round straw broom on a rough wood handle

Prop: an old-style round straw broom with a rough wooden handle

Costume: Bible-times costume

THE INNKEEPER'S WIFE enters, sweeping as she moves. She pauses and wipes her brow.

THE INNKEEPER'S WIFE: Whew! Has it been busy around here recently! Ever since Caesar Augustus issued that decree about a census being taken of the entire Roman world, we have had a mad house. Everyone has to go to the town of his ancestors to register, and I never realized how many people would have to return here to Bethlehem. Of course, I knew a lot of people were descendants of David, but have you ever thought about trying to find them all a place to sleep? My husband has spent so much time telling people he doesn't have any space left that he has been unable to get much work of any kind done. Not that I'm complaining. We can certainly use the extra money. I just want everything back to normal . . . *[staring into the distance]* although, I'm beginning to wonder if things will ever be like they were before. *[pausing and sweeping briefly before continuing]* Do you like to watch people? Well, you certainly meet a lot of interesting characters when you run an inn— some you would just as soon never meet again; some are just plain folks; and some are the kind you wouldn't mind having around for a while. Of course, occasionally you meet people that you know, beyond all doubt, you'll never forget. *[sweeping very briefly]* For instance, there was this one couple that came by late the other night. Sweetest looking girl you can ever imagine, but bless her heart, it was obvious she was going to have a baby anytime. Personally, I think it was absolutely awful that she had to make the journey from Nazareth in her condition, but that wasn't my call to make. Her husband seemed like a very caring and concerned man, and I could tell he did not know what they would do when my husband told him that not another soul could be squeezed into our inn. However, before they left, so obviously disappointed, my husband told the man they could sleep in the animal shelter, but that was the best he could do. *[pauses to sweep]* Do you ever think that sometimes things happen because that was the way they were meant to be? I personally believe it was a blessing that they ended up in the stable with the animals instead of in here with all those people. Wouldn't it have terrible for her to have her baby with so many strangers around? She had the baby sometime after they were settled in for the night. They made a bed in a manger after wrapping Him with pieces of cloth. That was not a night for much sleeping. The strangest things began occurring. People started noticing this bright star, unlike any they had ever seen before, and it seemed to settle right over our stable. *[The last four words are spoken with amazement, and each word is stressed slowly.]* Then these shepherds from nearby fields came, and you cannot believe what they shared. They were having a typical night until, all of a sudden, an angel from the Lord appeared to them and God's glory surrounded them. Naturally, they were half scared out of their wits, but the angel told them not to be afraid, that he had wonderful news for all people. He told them a Savior had just been born in the city of David, which, of course, is Bethlehem, and that this baby was Christ the Lord. The angel gave them a sign so they would know when they found the king. He said the baby would be wrapped in strips of cloth and lying in a manger. Several other angels then joined him, praising God. I remember the shepherds telling us that the angels declared, "Glory to God in the highest, and on earth peace to men on whom his favor rests." The shepherds wanted to find the baby, and that's when they came here—here to our inn. And they found baby Jesus, just as the angels said. Do you think it is possible? Do you believe this tiny baby could be our Savior? *[Exits, sweeping. Blackout.]*

Missing Out at Christmas

by John Cosper

Summary: A young couple, striving to have the perfect holiday, misses a dozen signs pointing them to the real story of Christmas.
Characters:
PHIL—newlywed
SUSAN—newlywed
ERIN KING—friend of SUSAN
RALPH KING—friend of SUSAN
JOSEPH KING—friend of SUSAN
Setting: the mall
Props: shopping bags full of gifts
Costumes: winter clothes, tacky Christmas sweaters for PHIL and SUSAN

PHIL and SUSAN enter, laughing together, carrying shopping bags.

SUSAN: Well, we've done it. Our first year as a couple, and we've finished all our Christmas shopping.
PHIL: We got everything?
SUSAN: We took care of your folks, my folks, your brother, your sister and her husband and their kids, my sister and her hubby and her kids . . .
PHIL: What did we get your nieces?
SUSAN: The baby dolls with the drinking bottles, remember?
PHIL: And what did you get me?
SUSAN: *[giggles]* I'm not telling.
PHIL: So, it's 4:30 on Christmas Eve. What's on the agenda now?
SUSAN: Well, we have dinner at my folks, then opening gifts, and then the party at Elaine's. Presents in the morning for you and me, then lunch at your folks' place, dinner with my folks, and another party at the Daniels' house. What's wrong?
PHIL: Well, I don't know. It just seems like something's missing. We saw all the movies, right?
SUSAN: We watched *It's A Wonderful Life* last night, *Home Alone* on Thanksgiving, *Rudolph* was last week, *Christmas Vacation* is at my parent's place tonight, *Christmas Story* after lunch tomorrow.
PHIL: What about *Charlie Brown*?

SUSAN: It was on when you were out of town last week, but I taped it for you.

PHIL: Good. But, you know, I still think we've missed something in this season. I wonder what that could be?

[The KINGS enter, carrying shopping bags full of gifts.]

SUSAN: Oh my goodness! Look who it is!

PHIL: Who?

SUSAN: It's the three Kings!

PHIL: Who?

SUSAN: My old friends from high school—the King family.

ERIN: Hey, Susan!

SUSAN: Hey, you guys! Phil, these are my friends the Kings—Erin, Ralph, and Joseph.

PHIL: I remember you. You all came to the wedding.

ERIN: Good to see you again, Phil.

RALPH: Merry Christmas.

PHIL: Merry Christmas to you.

SUSAN: Wow, seems like forever since we last saw each other. What are you doing up here?

JOSEPH: The usual last minute Christmas shopping.

ERIN: Bearing gifts for the newborn King.

PHIL: Excuse me?

RALPH: Joseph and his wife had a baby last week.

SUSAN: Ohhhhh, Joseph, congratulations!

JOSEPH: Thank you.

ERIN: You should see him, Susan. He's the cutest thing.

SUSAN: That's so wonderful. And how's Mary, Joseph?

JOSEPH: Well, she had a few complications in delivery and had a rough day or two, but everything's stable now.

SUSAN: I'm so glad.

RALPH: Oh, you will never believe who's in town visiting.

SUSAN: Who?

RALPH: The Shepherds!

SUSAN: Rob and Diane?

ERIN: Yes!

SUSAN: Wow, I haven't seen them in forever.

JOSEPH: Yeah, they came to see the baby after they heard about him from Gabriel.

SUSAN: Gabriel Roberts? Wow, there's someone else I haven't seen in a while.

JOSEPH: Well the Shepherds came in last night. They're staying with us too.

ERIN: They tried to get a room at the Holiday Inn, but it's Christmas so there is no room in the inn.

SUSAN: I'd love to see them.

PHIL: Well, maybe we can stop by.

JOSEPH: Oh, please do, yes. We'll all be staying at Mom and Dad's.

SUSAN: Oh, the one off Bethlehem Road?

JOSEPH: Yeah, that's it.

RALPH: Right behind the Lone Star Steakhouse.

ERIN: The one with the big, bright star out front.

PHIL: That shouldn't be hard to find.

JOSEPH: Yeah, if you're coming from the east, just follow Bethlehem Road til you see the star.

PHIL: Sounds good.

ERIN: Well, we need to get going, but maybe we'll see you later?

JOSEPH: Drop by any time. We'll catch you later. Merry Christmas.

PHIL & SUSAN: Merry Christmas.

[The KINGS exit.]

SUSAN: Wow, that was great.

PHIL: What a nice family.

SUSAN: So did you think of what we're missing?

PHIL: No, I didn't. It's probably something so obvious, we'll kick ourselves later.

SUSAN: I wonder what it could be.

[They both think and then eyes widen. They look at each other and snap fingers in unison.]

PHIL & SUSAN: *[shouting]* Candy Canes!

[Blackout.]

Missing Out at Christmas   15

Between Two Mothers

by Paula Reed

Summary: This sketch looks into the plans MARY might have had for her newborn baby. *[Related Scripture: Luke 1:26-38; Matthew 1:18-25]*
Characters:
MARY—young woman
TERAH—young woman
Costumes: Bible-times costumes

MARY and TERAH, walk in closely together, talking.

TERAH: I don't really know what to say! That the angel would deliver such a message to you is truly amazing!

MARY: I know it sounds incredible and it is amazing that the Lord would shine His favor upon me in such a way as this. It leaves me breathless and yet filled with wonder and joy. For me, a virgin, to be pregnant with the child of God is something I am just now beginning to grasp, but have yet to fully understand.

TERAH: I must confess it leaves me confused as well as a little frightened for you.

MARY: Frightened for me—why?

TERAH: Mary, surely you must know of the wagging tongues in our village. There are those who say you have brought disgrace to your family and should be stoned. That is why I had to find you and speak with you face-to-face.

MARY: Oh, Terah, you have always been such a loving and faithful friend! Please don't worry over me. While I may not know all of His plan, I am confident that the Lord will see me through, for the angel himself said to me, "Nothing is impossible with God."

TERAH: But what about Joseph? Does he believe that all you have told him is true?

MARY: He didn't at first—in fact he planned to break our betrothal quietly to save me from further shame and embarrassment. I believe he was deeply wounded thinking that maybe I had been with another man.

TERAH: And now?

MARY: He was also visited by a messenger of God and believes that
what has been foretold will come to pass. He has vowed to honor
our pledge and we will be married soon. Joseph is a righteous man,
for God has chosen him to be the father of His own Son and I am
honored to be his wife.

TERAH: Dear Mary, your faith has always been as deep as the sea. You
are truly God's humble servant—no wonder you have found such
favor with Him.

MARY: While I cannot fathom the mysteries of our Lord, I do believe
and trust in His purpose for my life. And your words are very
comforting to me, my friend. I will miss you while I am away visiting
my cousin, Elizabeth.

TERAH: As I will miss you. *[shyly]* And when you return I will have a
surprise for you as well!

MARY: A surprise? Terah, what is it? We have never kept secrets from
one another—please tell me!

TERAH: Simon didn't want me to say anything just yet, but . . . I, too,
am with child!

MARY: Terah! I am so happy for you and for Simon! And to think
that we will carry our children together brings me such joy! This is
wonderful news!

TERAH: We are so happy—our first child! We have such hopes and
dreams for this little one. But tell me, Mary, what does the mother of
the child of God hope for her son?

MARY: *[thoughtfully]* I suppose I am no different than you, Terah, or any
other mother for that matter. But to think and dream about His future
is more than my feeble mind can comprehend. Dare I think that I can
shape the destiny of the Son of the Most High? He is conceived of the
Holy Spirit but yet His life grows within me, a mere woman. I may
choose His sandals, but the Lord will direct His steps. When He cries,
I will dry His tears even though they will be the very tears of God; and
when He laughs, I will dance with joy at the sound of His voice. I am
not worthy of any of this, but I am willing, and I humbly accept God's
precious gift given to me.

TERAH: But, surely, you must wonder of His future. For what do you
suppose the angel meant when he said, "his kingdom will never end?"
Forgive me, Mary, but you are as poor as I—we have not the means,
or the resources, to build a village, let alone a kingdom.

MARY: What you say is true and of course I wonder—I wonder if His life will be marked with joy or with sorrow. I wonder what He will have to endure to bring salvation to our people as the prophets foretold many years ago. I do not know how the Lord intends to build His kingdom through His Son, Jesus—will it be with blood and tears or with power and might? I do not know what His future holds but somehow I know He holds our future. I do not know many things but I do know that I will love this baby boy and I will tenderly and lovingly care for this holy child of God.

TERAH: *[softly]* Perhaps that is all you need to know for now. You will be such a good mother.

MARY: As will you, Terah. And we will help each other when the nights are long and our days filled with the tasks of raising our children! But what about you, my friend? What do you dream for your unborn child?

TERAH: I hope that he will be healthy and strong and a kind and honest person. That he will remember the goodness of our Lord Jehovah and follow His commands. I pray that if there is a defining moment that changes his life, it will be for the good, not the bad. Of course, if he has a head for buying and selling like his father—that would be an added blessing!

MARY: *[laughing with her]* Are you already so convinced it is a son you carry?

TERAH: Simon desperately wishes for a son and has already chosen his name—if in fact it is a boy! He is to be called Judas—Judas Iscariot. Simon thinks it is a name of strength and power.

MARY: Judas it is then. May God bless you and Simon with a son and may he grow into your dreams for him.

TERAH: Who knows? Perhaps my son will serve your son, Jesus, in His new kingdom and together they will change all of history!

MARY: Maybe we go too far in our thinking, Terah! Perhaps our best response is to just trust in the creator to fulfill His promise as He determines. But now I must hurry and go see my cousin, Elizabeth. Take care, my friend, and I will see you soon.

TERAH: Goodbye, Mary, and may God be with you and Joseph in the days and months ahead.

[Blackout.]

The Girl Who Had Everything

by John Cosper

Summary: A spoiled little rich girl, who has every toy ever made, strikes out on a desperate search for the ultimate dolly that she does not have . . . and learns a lesson about giving at Christmastime.

Characters:

HENDERSON—CAROL's butler, older man with an English accent, acts as a NARRATOR to CAROL's actions in the story

JESSICA—a spoiled, rotten little girl, about age 6; can be played by adult dressed as child

BUDDY—JESSICA's friend, about 6 years old; can be played by adult dressed as a child

SANTA CLAUS

TONY—commercial guy, middle-aged, very sneaky personality

TOY SELLER—mysterious older man

Props: toy T. Rex dinosaur, a bucket and pail, a doll, little boy's coat, sales counter (can use a desk) with a cash register or cash box on it, shiny paper star

Costumes: little girl dress for JESSICA, tux for HENDERSON, kid clothes for BUDDY, Santa suit, suit and tie for TONY, old-fashioned shopkeeper clothes for the TOY SELLER

HENDERSON enters.

HENDERSON: Merry Christmas, children! And how are all of you? Is everyone here ready for Christmas? I bet you are! We're certainly ready at my house. Not that I have a family of my own. You see, I'm the butler to a very special girl who . . . well, before I tell you about her, let me ask a question. What do you want for Christmas? *[Get responses from the kids.]* Wow, those are all great gifts. But let me ask you this . . . if you had ALL those things, if you had EVERY toy and plaything in the world, what would you ask for? This is a story about a girl who had to answer such a question. It's the story of a little girl named Carol.

JESSICA: *[offstage]* Is that my cue?

HENDERSON: Yes it is, Miss.

[JESSICA enters.]

JESSICA: Hi, everybody! My name's Jessica and I'm in a play! This is MY play!

HENDERSON: Miss Jessica, can we go on with the story?

JESSICA: *Fine*, Henderson! I was just trying to make friends.

HENDERSON: Jessica's parents were very loving, and they were extremely rich. In fact they were so rich . . . tell them Jessica.

JESSICA: I had every toy ever made in the whole wide world!

HENDERSON: Yes, Jessica had everything. And by everything, I mean every toy ever known to kid-dom. Teddy bears?

JESSICA: Got 'em.

HENDERSON: Toy ponies?

JESSICA: Got 'em.

HENDERSON: Dolls, babies, bottles, strollers?

JESSICA: Every last one of 'em.

HENDERSON: Video game stations?

JESSICA: All of them.

HENDERSON: Bicycles?

JESSICA: Every color you can imagine!

HENDERSON: Robots and soldiers?

JESSICA: Eww!!!

HENDERSON: I said, Robots and soldiers?

JESSICA: I heard you, Henderson. I've got 'em. They're stupid, but boy, do I have 'em.

HENDERSON: Yes, she even had every boy's toy ever made—soldiers, squirt guns, balls, sporting equipment, rockets, blocks . . . Jessica had toys in every room of the house, and there were quite a few rooms.

JESSICA: One hundred and six, to be exact!

HENDERSON: And she played with every one of those toys.

JESSICA: A played with toy is a happy toy. And I believe in keeping my toys happy.

HENDERSON: And, I might add, Jessica believed in sharing. Every afternoon, her friends would come over and want to play. And Jessica always let them.

JESSICA: Yes, but sometimes, they had to play by certain rules.

[BUDDY enters.]

BUDDY: Hi, Jessica!
JESSICA: Hi, Buddy. What's up?
BUDDY: I was wonderin' if I could play with some of the toys.
JESSICA: The Barbie dolls?
BUDDY: NO!!
JESSICA: Polly Pockets?
BUDDY: You know which ones I want!
JESSICA: Ohhhh . . . I bet you wanna see THESE toys!

[JESSICA pulls out a toy dinosaur].

BUDDY: Wow! That's a T. Rex?
JESSICA: It is? OK. Sure.
BUDDY: Can I have him?
JESSICA: OK, but he has to play tea party with my Disney Princesses!
BUDDY: Ick! No way! We're gonna go capture wimpy dinosaurs and eat them!
JESSICA: Gross!
BUDDY: Please???
JESSICA: OK. But first, you gotta say T. Rex is a dollie.
BUDDY: I'm not saying that.
JESSICA: Say he's a dollie.
BUDDY: He's not a dollie. He's an action figure!
JESSICA: Dollie!
BUDDY: Action figure!
JESSICA: Dollie!
BUDDY: Action figure!
JESSICA: You want to play with him?
BUDDY: Yes!
JESSICA: Then say he's a dollie! Come on, do it!
BUDDY: No!
JESSICA: Say he's a dollie!
BUDDY: No!
JESSICA: Say it! Say T. Rex is a dollie! Say it! Say it!
BUDDY: OK, he's a dollie, he's a dollie! Just give it!
JESSICA: OK. Here you go.

The Girl Who Had Everything   21

[BUDDY takes the dinosaur and runs off.]

JESSICA: I just love doing that.

HENDERSON: Jessica had more than toys to share with her friends. She had bicycles, motorized cars, wagons, a swing set and jungle gym, teeter-totters, a merry-go-round, a king-size ball pit, and a swimming pool.

JESSICA: *[giggles]* Yeah, and I got these really cool swimmies for when I go in the pool so I don't go *[making drowning sounds]* glug-glug-glug.

HENDERSON: And right beside the pool, the world's largest, biggest, most enormous sandbox!

JESSICA: The sandbox! Good grief, Henderson, do you know how long it's been since I was in the sandbox?

HENDERSON: It has been a while, Miss.

JESSICA: We gotta do something about that!

[JESSICA grabs a bucket and pail.]

JESSICA: Come on! I'm gonna bury you up to your neck.

HENDERSON: I'm afraid we can't do that, Miss.

JESSICA: You gettin' an attitude with me, Henderson?

HENDERSON: No, Miss. It's simply that it is too cold to play outside.

JESSICA: Aw, baloney!

HENDERSON: It's December. And the temperature has dropped well below—

JESSICA: *[smacking HENDERSON's arm]* Did you say December?

HENDERSON: Yes, Miss.

JESSICA: Good grief!! Don't you know what that means? It's *Christmas*!

HENDERSON: Indeed, it is.

JESSICA: I don't believe it. It snuck up on me! We've gotta go see Santa Claus!

HENDERSON: And so it came to pass, that I took Jessica to the mall, and she went to see the great bearded wonder, Santa Claus.

JESSICA: I can't believe Henderson letting me forget what time of year it is. No dessert for him tonight! Well, maybe just a taste.

[SANTA enters.]

SANTA: Ho, ho, ho! Merry Christmas!

JESSICA: It's Santa! It's Santa!

SANTA: And what's your name, little girl?

JESSICA: Jessica.

SANTA: Hello, Jessica. Have you been a good girl this year?

JESSICA: Yes.

SANTA: You know, I have a list, and I'm going to check it twice.

JESSICA: And I'll be on it both times or you'll hear from my lawyer.

SANTA: Well, we don't need to bring any of those naughty people into the picture. Tell me what you want for Christmas!

JESSICA: OK. I want . . . I want . . .

SANTA: Yes?

JESSICA: Hang on, give me a minute.

SANTA: OK, but remember, Santa has to have time to hear all these other boys and girls.

JESSICA: Don't rush me, OK. Let me think. OK, how about a—no, I've got that. What about—no, I have three of those. Maybe a nice—no. Or maybe . . .

SANTA: Anytime, kid.

JESSICA: Good grief . . . I don't know what to ask Santa to bring me for Christmas!!

HENDERSON: Yes, it was quite a dilemma for the girl who had everything. Because you see, when you have *everything* . . . there's not much left to ask for.

JESSICA: Now you tell me this! I can't believe it. Christmas is going to come, and I'm not going to get anything. And I was really, really GOOD this year!

HENDERSON: No argument here.

JESSICA: You're STILL not getting a big dessert tonight.

HENDERSON: Sad.

JESSICA: Well, let's eliminate some categories. I've got ALL the toys there are to have. Including the ones I hate. All the video games. And hard as it is to believe, more dresses than I could ever possibly wear, even if I changed clothes four times a day.

HENDERSON: Which she does.

JESSICA: Shush!

HENDERSON: Perhaps, Miss, you should think outside the box. Think of something more unusual and exotic.

JESSICA: Like what?

HENDERSON: Perhaps you could ask for your own boy band.

JESSICA: Hey, that's a great—Nah! I'd only have to feed and clean up after them.

HENDERSON: A task which would no doubt fall to me. But I would be willing to help if you really wanted your very own boy band.

JESSICA: Henderson, if you want a boy band member so much, YOU ask for it.

HENDERSON: I would, Miss, except this is not a play about me. It's all about you.

JESSICA: A play? You mean there's a play about me?

HENDERSON: Yes, Miss. We're in it even as we speak.

JESSICA: Oh no!

HENDERSON: What's the matter.

JESSICA: I was gonna ask Santa for a play that was all about me. But I've already got one of those too!

HENDERSON: So the search began. Carol used her daddy's computer, built a database, and tried to discover some toy, gift she did not have.

JESSICA: This is hopeless!

HENDERSON: I'm sure you'll think of something, Miss.

JESSICA: No, not the Christmas present. The computer, I don't get it. It's stupid! Where's Buddy? He usually knows how to work these things.

HENDERSON: Why don't we skip that part of the story and cut to where you see the commercial for the *ultimate* toy.

JESSICA: The *ultimate* toy??

[TONY enters with the Julie doll tucked in his suit jacket and stands off to the side of the stage to make a TV announcement. JESSICA stares at him as if he is on her TV.]

TONY: Hey, kids, looking for the perfect gift for Christmas?

JESSICA: Yes!

TONY: Tired of the same old same old?

JESSICA: Am I ever!

TONY: This Christmas, your dream is going to come true.

JESSICA: I'm going to get to sing with Gwen Stefani???

TONY: You're going to find a special gift under your tree, a little doll we call the *Ultimate Julie Doll*!

[*TONY pulls out a Julie doll.*]

JESSICA: The Julie Doll? I got a million of those!

TONY: Not like this one, you don't!

JESSICA: Oh yeah? What makes her so special?

TONY: Ultimate Julie Doll is the greatest doll ever made. She has her own bottle to drink from.

JESSICA: Been there, done that!

TONY: And she has special tear ducts! This dollie actually cries!

JESSICA: Yawn! Tell me something I don't know!

TONY: She can even wet her diapers!

JESSICA: Yeah, yeah, old material! Come on, show me something *really* new!

TONY: She can even make all the little boys cry!

JESSICA: She *what*?

TONY: That's right, the Ultimate Julie Doll drinks, wets, cries, and makes all the boys cry!

JESSICA: No kiddin?

TONY: How long have you waited for a doll that not only drinks, wets, and cries, but can make all the boys cry?

JESSICA: My whole life!

TONY: Then you know how much you're going to hate yourself if you don't get the Ultimate Julie Doll for Christmas!

JESSICA: Do I ever!

TONY: Life just won't be complete without it!

JESSICA: You're telling me!

TONY: So be sure and ask your mom and dad for the Ultimate Julie Doll!

JESSICA: Good grief! It's only a few day til' Christmas too! Henderson!

HENDERSON: Yes, Miss?

JESSICA: Henderson, we have a crisis! I have to have the Ultimate Julie Doll for Christmas!

HENDERSON: Don't you already have a hundred Julie dolls?

JESSICA: Not the *Ultimate* Julie Doll!

HENDERSON: The Ultimate Julie Doll? What makes her so Ultimate?

JESSICA: She drinks, she wets, she cries, *and* she makes all the boys cry!

HENDERSON: Impossible!

JESSICA: It's true! It's true! Henderson . . . I've gotta have that doll!

HENDERSON: What shall we do, Miss?

JESSICA: I need to see Santa!

HENDERSON: Of course.

JESSICA: Well, hurry up with the costume change!! Go, go, go!

[SANTA enters.]

SANTA: Ho, ho, ho, Merry—

JESSICA: Skip it, Santa! We got business to take care of!

SANTA: Of course. What do you want?

JESSICA: Santa, OK, I know what I want and this is *really, really* important!!

SANTA: I'm sure. What is it, Carol?

JESSICA: Santa, I have to have the Ultimate Julie Doll!

SANTA: The Julie Doll?

JESSICA: That's right, I need the Julie Doll! The one that drinks, wets, cries, AND can make all the boys cry?

SANTA: Yes, I know the doll.

JESSICA: Please say you can get me one, Santa! Please, please!

SANTA: I wish I could, Jessica, but . . .

JESSICA: But what?

SANTA: Jessica, it's impossible.

JESSICA: No, it's not.

SANTA: Yes, it is! Every little girl in the world wants that doll, but it's the most rare doll in the world.

JESSICA: How rare?

SANTA: Well, Jessica, the Julie Doll Company factory burned down after they started running the commercials. They only saved *one* doll.

JESSICA: Well, I have to have it!I don't believe this! What is this world coming to? A little girl is good all year, in the hopes that she'll make Santa's nice list, because she knows Santa only brings gifts to the good boys and girls. Then, after a hard year of being good, she expects that Santa will bring her everything she wants . . . only to be disappointed, crushed, destroyed. *[begins to throw a fit]* Why, Santa? Why?! Why?!

SANTA: *[offers her candy]* Candy cane?

JESSICA: Get outta here, Santa!!

HENDERSON: Jessica was heartbroken, but not even Santa could discourage her in her quest.

JESSICA: I've gotta have that doll! Henderson, we're not going to eat or sleep until we find it!

HENDERSON: Are you sure that's a wise decision?

JESSICA: OK, we can stop for a hamburger, but only at supper time!

HENDERSON: *[rolls his eyes and begins in a low, TV Announcer-type tone]* And so the search for the Ultimate Julie Doll began. Jessica searched high and low, in every toy store in town.

JESSICA: Julie! *[She runs frantically around stage looking behind, under, around everything.]*

HENDERSON: She searched in every Wal-Mart®, K-Mart®, S-Mart, Q-Mart, pretty much covered all the "Marts."

JESSICA: Julie!

HENDERSON: She searched to the north and the south!

JESSICA: Julie!

HENDERSON: She searched in the east and the west!

JESSICA: Julie!

HENDERSON: She searched over in that part of the room.

JESSICA: *[runs to that part of the stage]* Julie!

HENDERSON: She searched in that little boy's coat!

JESSICA: *[looking in the coat]* Julie!

HENDERSON: And she searched in that little girl's purse!

JESSICA: *[looking in the purse]* Julie!

HENDERSON: How about if we skip to the next part of the story where you learn about the one Ultimate Julie Doll and who bought it?

JESSICA: We find the Julie doll?

HENDERSON: That's right, we do!

JESSICA: Then gimme it!

HENDERSON: I don't have it. It was sold by a mysterious old toy seller.

JESSICA: What mysterious old toy seller?

[The Toy Seller enters and walks up to the sales counter that should already be on a side of the stage. Jessica and Henderson walk up to counter.]

Toy Seller: Hi, I'm the Mysterious old toy seller. Can I interest you in a Christmas gift?

Jessica: I want the Ultimate Julie Doll!

Toy Seller: Lots of little girls want that doll.

Jessica: Yes, but it's *my* doll! I need it! It's the only toy I don't have! Please, please, oh *please*!

Toy Seller: I wish I could give it to you, but . . .

Jessica: Here we go again.

Toy Seller: I sold it already to another little girl.

Jessica: No! Say it isn't so!

Toy Seller: It's so.

Jessica: *[screams]* NOOOOOOOOOOOOOOOOOOOOOOO . . .

[Jessica continues her scream. She pauses, looks at the Toy seller, then resumes screaming.]

Jessica: NOOOOOOOOOOOOOOOOOOOOOOOOOOOOOOO!

Toy Seller: You done?

Jessica: Yes. No, wait, NOOOOOOOOOOOOOOOOO… OK. I'm better.

Toy Seller: Good.

Jessica: I can live without that doll. I have so many others.

Toy Seller: You don't need anymore?

Jessica: Of course not. I have lots of dolls that drink and wet and cry.

Toy Seller: Then don't worry about it.

Jessica: But I don't have one that will make all the boys cry! HENDERSON!

Henderson: Yes, Miss?

Jessica: The mysterious old toy seller sold my doll.

Henderson: Shall we alert the military?

Jessica: Will it get me my doll?

Henderson: No. Well, I am so sorry to hear about the Ultimate Julie Doll. I guess we're just going to have to make do with—

Jessica: Henderson! You're not giving up, are you?

Henderson: Miss Carol, there's only one thing left to do.

JESSICA: Exactly. We gotta find the girl who has my doll and buy it off her!

HENDERSON: How will we pay for it?

JESSICA: We'll sell all those stupid boy toys!

HENDERSON: Very well. But how do we find your doll?

JESSICA: Is this my play?

HENDERSON: Yes.

JESSICA: Is it going to have a happy ending?

HENDERSON: I think it is.

JESSICA: Then I guess in the next scene we'll find the doll, won't we?

HENDERSON: I guess we will.

JESSICA: So let's get there.

HENDERSON: And so we did. We searched all over the mysterious old toy seller's town and came upon a small church. Carol was very tired by this point, and so was I. So we sat down to watch the play they were doing.

JESSICA: A play within a play? What is this—*Hamlet*?

HENDERSON: The play began to unfold, and Carol saw strange sights.

JESSICA: Wow.

[HENDERSON begins picking people out of the audience to portray the characters in the nativity scene as he names them.]

HENDERSON: She saw shepherds with their sheep.

JESSICA: Fake! Those sheep are fake!

HENDERSON: Haven't you heard of suspension of disbelief?

JESSICA: Haven't these actors heard of *real* props?

HENDERSON: She also saw three kings bearing gifts.

JESSICA: Do they have the Ultimate Julie Doll?

HENDERSON: No, Miss Jessica. They've got gold, frankincense, and myrrh.

JESSICA: Eww, I don't like Frankincense, he's scary.

HENDERSON: She also saw a beautiful angel.

JESSICA: Wow! Look, she's so pretty!

HENDERSON: All of these unique characters were gathered in a barn.

JESSICA: Was there a cow?

HENDERSON: Uh, no. Not for this scene.

JESSICA: I want there to be a cow, Henderson! Pick out a cow!

HENDERSON: Fine. There was a cow.

JESSICA: I like cows.

HENDERSON: And in the center of it all, she saw two more characters. A young man named Joseph. And a young lady named Mary.

[HENDERSON puts the Ultimate Julie Doll in Mary's arms.]

JESSICA: HENDERSON!

HENDERSON: Yes, Miss?

JESSICA: That's her! That's my doll!

HENDERSON: I know, Miss.

JESSICA: We have to go get her! *[clinches her teeth and stomps her feet]* Get her NOW!

HENDERSON: We can't, Miss. Not in the middle of the play.

JESSICA: Noooo, this play is stupid!

HENDERSON: Jessica, I'm surprised. Don't you know what this play is about?

JESSICA: No.

HENDERSON: Well, it just so happens we're at the part where you'll find out. *[paraphrased from Luke 2 and Matthew 2]* Joseph went to Bethlehem, the town of David. He went there with Mary, who was pledged to be married to him and expecting a child. While they were there, the time came for the baby to be born, and she gave birth to her firstborn, a son. She wrapped him in cloths and placed Him in a manger, because there was no room for them in the inn.

JESSICA: No room in the inn? That's so sad. The baby should be in a hospital!

HENDERSON: I know He should, but this was the way Jesus chose to enter the world.

JESSICA: Jesus? You mean the Ultimate Julie Doll is playing *Jesus*?

HENDERSON: That's right, Jessica, the Son of God who was born on Christmas.

JESSICA: Wow! But what about all these other people?

HENDERSON: These are the people who witnessed the birth of Jesus. An angel appeared to the shepherds and told them where to find the baby. And then the three kings followed a bright star to see the baby.

JESSICA: I didn't see any star.

[HENDERSON pulls a star from his suit pocket.]

HENDERSON: You see, Jessica, the reason we have Christmas is because of Jesus.

JESSICA: Ooh, I get it! And the reason we have presents is because the kings brought Him Frankenstein!

HENDERSON: Well, the three kings brought Him gifts. But the real gift was Jesus himself. He was sent from Heaven to die for our sins so that we could know Him and have a relationship with God.

JESSICA: Wow! One little baby did all that?

HENDERSON: He did indeed.

JESSICA: Wow.

HENDERSON: *(to audience)* It was at that moment that something clicked inside Jessica.

JESSICA: Henderson, I don't want that doll any more.

HENDERSON: But Miss Jessica, she drinks, she wets, she cries, and she makes all the little boys cry.

JESSICA: But Henderson, Jesus started Christmas, and He came to *give*, not to *get* presents. I don't want to get anything now. I want to give things away, just like Jesus.

HENDERSON: That sounds like a very good idea.

JESSICA: *[shrugs and nods]* I know. I thought of it. Thanks.

HENDERSON: And so, we returned home, and Jessica began to wrap up her toys. *[HENDERSON looks at JESSICA.]* Everyone was amazed at the change in Jessica. And everywhere she went, people just had to ask her… Why are you giving away so many gifts for Christmas?

JESSICA: Because Christmas is about the greatest gift of all—the love of Jesus!

HENDERSON: Thanks to Jessica, it was a very Merry Christmas. And everyone who met her got to hear the good news that Jesus Christ was born on Christmas Day! The end!

JESSICA: *[stomps foot]* Hey, that's my line. *[realizes she was mean]* Oh, sorry Henderson. Good job. And Merry Christmas! *[to audience]* The end. *[smiles and curtsies]*

[Blackout.]

The Lamplighter
by Lori Stanley Roeleveld

Summary: WILLIAM, disheartened and seeking answers on Christmas Eve falls asleep after watching *A Christmas Carol* and dreams that he has been transported back to a simpler time. Through a series of exchanges, he discovers that his questions haven't changed—and neither have the answers.

Characters:

WILLIAM —a troubled young man

LAMPLIGHTER /LUKE FREEMAN —Victorian lamplighter

FELICITY —flighty young woman holiday shopping

RALPH —good-natured young man out for holiday merrymaking

PROFESSOR HIGHBROW —arrogant teacher, disinterested in Christmas

FREDERICK —flustered father

SYLVIA—FREDERICK's harried wife

CHILDREN and CHURCHGOERS —several nonspeaking roles for background

Setting: opens in a modern bedroom but action takes place in a Victorian England churchyard

Props: bed, TV, telephone, at least 2 street lamps, holiday decorations, church steps and door, a bench, sounds of church bells

Costumes: pajamas for WILLIAM in the opening and closing scenes, Victorian outdoor winter clothing for everyone in all other scenes

WILLIAM sits in bed watching the end of A Christmas Carol. *He is on the phone. From the TV we hear Tiny Tim say "And God bless us everyone!"*

WILLIAM: *[talking into the phone]* OK, sis, I've watched *A Christmas Carol*. Are you happy? No, I'm still not getting warm fuzzies about Christmas. Life is a mess and I don't see that God has any answers so I'm not planning to show up at His house! *[pause]* Yeah, well, Dickens lived in simpler times. He never had to wrestle with the issues we do. If he had, he'd have stuck with "Bah humbug" as his message. *[pause]* Look, you pray enough for both of us. I doubt I'd be really welcome in God's house. Gotta get some sleep. I'll talk with you tomorrow and, no, I won't be at church!

[WILLIAM *goes to sleep. When he wakes up, he is in Victorian times, dressed like a Dickens's character, at the bottom of the steps of a church.* WILLIAM *will need time for a costume change here. Church bells are ringing and people are entering the church for service. The* LAMPLIGHTER *passes through, lighting the street lamps. The* LAMPLIGHTER *struggles with one lamp for a moment but eventually moves on, leaving it unlit.* WILLIAM *sits on a bench. He seems confused. People greet him as if they know him. He pinches himself a couple of times.* FELICITY *and her friend, laden with packages and talking excitedly, come along.* FELICITY *spots* WILLIAM *and motions her friend to go on without her.*]

FELICITY: [*piercingly, excitedly*] Good evening, William. I certainly hope you're not planning to go into service looking like that!

WILLIAM: Good evening to you, miss. What's wrong with what I'm wearing?

FELICITY: Not those, silly! Your face! Why, you look positively forlorn. Don't you know it's Christmas Eve? Darling, *nobody* is sad on Christmas Eve! Why, it's simply not . . . Christian! What could you possibly have to be sad about tonight?

WILLIAM: Well . . . [*He tries to speak but she chatters on.*]

FELICITY: You look as though you could use a good dinner and a change of clothes. Times are hard. Well, buck up, sir. It is Christmas Eve and we can't have sad faces among the holiday decorations, can we?

WILLIAM: Well . . .

FELICITY: Dear William, after all, it's Christmas! Music. Decorations. Food. Gifts. Oooo, the gifts! I love getting gifts! It *is* what Christmas is all about.

WILLIAM: What is that, miss? Who are you again? What is Christmas all about?

FELICITY: Oh silly, It's Felicity. And Christmas is about happiness, dear boy, happiness! The Christmas spirit and all that. 'Tis a time for light and joyous spirits. There are 364 days a year to be maudlin and dreary but only one Christmas! We have so much, after all.

WILLIAM: But what if we didn't?

FELICITY: What do you mean?

WILLIAM: What if we had no money for gifts or not enough food for even a small feast? What if we had none of it to bring us happiness? What would Christmas be about then?

FELICITY: *[pausing for only a moment]* Oh, William, you absolutely wear me out! Please, no philosophy or dreary nonsense tonight. Do put on a good face if you plan to attend service, dear heart. Think happy thoughts, tidings of comfort and joy, tra-la.

WILLIAM: *[gesturing toward the church]* Aren't you going in?

FELICITY: *[with a giggle]* Oh, I'll go twice next week. I've so much to do! Gifts still to wrap, decorations. I've just no time! It's Christmas Eve, you know!

[FELICITY exits. WILLIAM looks up at the church. RALPH enters.]

RALPH: William! Willie boy!

WILLIAM: Good evening, sir!

RALPH: *[mimics him]* Good evening, sir. Well, aren't we formal tonight! Come on, William, it's Christmas Eve. We're on holiday. We're free! What are you doing here! Have your parents joined you here in London?

WILLIAM: No, I'm alone.

RALPH: You're in London alone and you're to spend your time in church praying. Oh, aren't you just a precious pride to your mum and dad. It looks like I got here just in time. Come to Clancy's tavern. We'll have ourselves the Christmas celebration we deserve!

WILLIAM: I don't know. I'm not really up for the tavern.

RALPH: What's wrong with you? What's a merry Christmas without some merrymaking? A little party is quite in keeping with the spirit of the holiday.

[PROFESSOR HIGHBROW enters the square.]

RALPH: Whoa! There's Professor Highbrow. The very sight of him puts a damper on my Christmas spirit. Well, I'm off, Willie boy. You should join us when you're done speaking with the Almighty! Give the Lord my regards and tell him I wish His Son a happy birthday. I'll be offering up a toast to the swaddled lad and to you as well, my friend!

[RALPH exits.]

PROFESSOR: Good evening to you, Master William.

WILLIAM: Good evening to you, professor. Are you attending Christmas services?

PROFESSOR: Why, I'll have none of this church rubbish on Christmas Eve or any night. Master William, you're not one of my better students but I never took you for someone who prescribed to ancient myths.

WILLIAM: Sir?

PROFESSOR: Well, all this treacle love and obedience, really! Spending hours on one's knees with angels attending is fine for women and children, perhaps even for old men who fear death but most of us in the academic community aspire to a greater intellectual enlightenment. Certainly even belief in the existence of a higher being is a preposterous notion. Why Mr. Darwin's theories of evolution are proving there is no need for us to rely on this archaic idea any longer. There is no proof of God, no evidence. Surely you have at least gleaned enough education to tell the truth from a fairy tale, have you not, young man?

WILLIAM: Well . . .

PROFESSOR: I suggest that you not spend this outdated holiday sitting amongst the uninformed trying to communicate with a being that does not exist and would not care about a mite such as you if He did. Find yourself a more intellectually stimulating occupation for the evening.

WILLIAM: Yes, sir.

[PROFESSOR exits. WILLIAM leans against the unlit lamp. FREDERICK and SYLVIA enter with their numerous children. They argue back and forth as they proceed toward the church steps. Their children are bickering, pinching, whining. Both parents are breaking up the children's fighting, wiping noses, straightening hair, reprimanding, etc. As they enter the church, FREDERICK hangs back and closes the door behind them. He takes off his hat and wipes his head with his handkerchief. He spots WILLIAM.]

FREDERICK: Ho there, lad! Good Christmas to you!

WILLIAM: Is it, sir?

FREDERICK: *[with false exuberance]* Children are a blessing, young man, a rich and bountiful blessing from God. That's what my wife tells me. It says so in the Good Book. Yes, those blessed little cherubs are what Christmas is all about, don't you know?

WILLIAM: Children, sir?

FREDERICK: Christmas is for children, don't you know? Me, I'm too old for magic and toys and following stars in the sky. Why Christmas would be just another day for me if it weren't for the joy of watching the wee ones open their gifts and enjoying the fine meal my Sylvia will prepare. Then, of course, we will spend the afternoon surrounded by the precious sound of the children playing, visiting with the in-laws and listening to Sylvia's beautiful voice as she goes on and on about how fortunate we are.

WILLIAM: So this is where you find your Christmas comfort and joy— then, in your wife and children?

FREDERICK: *[dryly]* You're not married, are you, lad?

[WILLIAM shakes his head no.]

FREDERICK: Yes, yes, that's every man's comfort in the holidays.

[SYLVIA sticks her head out of the church door and calls out in a shrill tone.]

SYLVIA: Frederick! Get in here this instant and help me control your children. What are you doing out there? This is Christmas Eve, don't you know? This is a time for family and your family is in here!

[SYLVIA exits. With a wink and a shrug, FREDERICK enters the church.]

WILLIAM: *[to himself]* Maybe there were never simpler times. Maybe people have always wrestled with getting up those church steps.

[WILLIAM considers entering the church. The streets are quiet now except for the sound of the church service just beginning. The LAMPLIGHTER is making his way home, checking each lamp once more on his way by. WILLIAM starts up the steps but backs down. He starts up the steps again but backs down a second time. He is unaware that LUKE THE

LAMPLIGHTER has stopped what he is doing and is leaning on the lit lamppost observing him.]

LUKE: Steps too high for you, son?

WILLIAM: What? *[looks at the steps]* Oh, those. No, thank you, sir, I was just deciding whether or not to go inside.

LUKE: Have you got a name?

WILLIAM: William.

LUKE: *[shaking WILLIAM's hand]* Luke Freeman. Pleased to make your acquaintance. Can you tell me, William, what factors weigh into your decision?

WILLIAM: I've had invitations to go elsewhere.

LUKE: True enough, there are many other options.

WILLIAM: The truth is I feel I just don't belong in there.

LUKE: *[sizes him up]* Belong, huh? Yes, well, maybe you don't.

[WILLIAM straightens up in surprise then slumps back down.]

WILLIAM: So you see I'm not good enough to be in there.

LUKE: Good enough? Is that what you think the problem is? Thinking you have to be good enough to get into the church, why, that's like thinking you aren't well enough to be admitted to hospital!

WILLIAM: Isn't that what it's all about? Being good?

LUKE: Humbug! There aren't any good people in there. Fact is, if someone showed up who was good enough, he might just muck up the deal for the rest of us!

WILLIAM: Oh, I get it. You mean it's not about being good; it's about trying to be good.

LUKE: I don't mean that at all. Try to be good? Why that'd be as useful as trying to be a cow!

WILLIAM: I don't understand.

LUKE: See, I could sincerely want to be a cow. I could try with all my heart and soul to be a cow. I could walk around a pasture on all fours, eat grass and moo with the best of them. Now I might convince myself I was a cow. I might even fool some others into thinking I was a cow. But soon as the farmer comes around for milking time, well, then the jig'd be up, wouldn't it now?

WILLIAM: *[skeptically]* But if it's not about being good, what is it about?

LUKE: What do you think about when you think about Christmas?
WILLIAM: Gifts, I guess . . .
LUKE: There you go! You already know the answer, lad!

[LUKE starts to walk away.]

WILLIAM: Wait, no, I don't understand! What do gifts and church have to do with each other?

[LUKE turns back.]

LUKE: [contemplates WILLIAM for a moment.] It is that we walk into that church knowing we are beggars, knowing we are not good enough to be in the presence of the Almighty. But rather than toss us out on our ear, as well He might, He laid out His very best before us! He offers all He has to us and that freely. Then in our very souls we know that He receives us to Him not because of who we are but because of who He is! Through His Son, we receive a goodness that is not our own and that is our inheritance!
WILLIAM: [pause] Sir, do the people in there [pointing toward the church] know about this? It sounds beautiful and wonderful but are you sure you got it right? No disrespect, Mr. Freeman, but I *know* some of those people and well . . . I just don't see it like you do.

[Meanwhile, LUKE has given his attention to a nearby lamp.]

LUKE: Do you see this lamp, son?

[WILLIAM nods.]

LUKE: That flame inside, that light, it is a wondrous thing! So beautiful to behold, it burns with amazing power. That flame gives warmth, light, and guidance but it also contains a mighty force with the power to consume.
WILLIAM: Yes, but I don't see . . .

LUKE: The problem with these lamps, see, is that they begin to collect dust and dirt. Some of them invite soot. If they aren't tended, the light dims so you'd think it wasn't even there. Truth is, though, that the light remains untouched, pure and blazing bright. One swipe of a rag and there is the beauty and purpose again!

WILLIAM: That's sort of interesting, but I don't see . . .

[LUKE turns to the unlit lamp.]

LUKE: Now, this lamp over here is a sad thing. Something is wrong with this one. It refuses to light. It doesn't matter how clean this lamp gets; it cannot give light on its own. Now it's fine for dressing up at Christmas but it was designed for more. *[He turns to WILLIAM with intensity.]*

WILLIAM: Are you about to tell me the Christmas story?

LUKE: *[passionate, intense]* You know the story, boy! That manger babe grew up and became a man like us but more than us. He was man and He was God. He gave His life in your place. He rose from the dead! He is that light! He is that flame burning in me. Sometimes I let the dust of my life dim that flame but in His forgiveness, I am clean. He shines through me once more, and I am whole because that is my purpose, my design. *[He pauses and turns to the unlit lamp.]* Look closely, son. Tonight you are this lamp. It is dark all around you, William, because you refuse to be lit from within. Have I helped at all with your decision, lad?

[Lights dim, when they come on, WILLIAM is waking up in his bed, back in his pajamas. He checks the time on his clock and picks up his phone.]

WILLIAM: Sis, hey, I caught you. What day is this? Really, do I still have time to make it to church? *[pause]* Yeah, don't ask, I'll just be there, OK? Oh, merry Christmas, sis. *[He hangs up.]* And God bless us everyone!

[Blackout.]

What Child Is This?

by John Cosper

Summary: MARY recalls the events that led up to her giving birth to
Jesus and wonders why she was chosen and how she will live up to
the calling.
Character:
MARY—the mother of Jesus
Setting: Bethlehem
Costume: Bible-times costumes

MARY is at center stage.

MARY: Look at him. He's just the most precious thing, isn't he? I
always knew he had a soft touch, but . . . the way he holds that baby
is amazing. I don't think I've ever seen him wearing a face like that.
Not even when he's holding me. I always knew Joseph would be a
great father. I just never dreamed it would happen this way. *[looks
up]* But no one but You could have dreamed up the year I've had.
It began simply enough. Well, I say simply, but having an angel
appear in your house is not an every day occurrence. "Greetings,
you who are highly favored. The Lord is with you." I remember
falling to my knees and at the same time pinching myself, thinking
I was dreaming. I wasn't, of course, and the angel told me what
was to happen. I would bear a son. He would be the Son of God,
conceived by the Holy Spirit. "May it be to me as you have said," I
consented. Not that I had any power over the situation. If anything,
I might have suggested choosing a more noble or well to do woman
for the job, but . . . I mean you don't question an angel, do you? I
was excited, and ran to tell my cousin Elizabeth about it. She was
bearing a promised child just as I was, a boy named John. But
after that visit, reality set in. How was I going to tell Joseph? What
would people think when they found out I was with child? And what
would they do? Only a year earlier, another girl in Nazareth had
become pregnant out of wedlock. She was taken outside town and
stoned. I believed that you would protect me, but . . . it didn't stop
me from becoming very afraid. A few days after I was visited by the

angel, I told Joseph. He just sat there, silent, not knowing what to say. I could tell part of him wanted to believe me, but . . . well, I understand why he couldn't. He left and I didn't see him for several days. I found out he was planning to break our engagement quietly, so as not to disgrace me. That told me that he really loved me, and it made it all that much harder to think of losing him. I needed my Joseph if I was to become a mother so young. You knew that and sent an angel to tell him the same news you told me. You also gave him our son's name: Jesus, the deliverer. The Messiah. Instead of a quiet divorce, we had a quiet wedding. And not a moment too soon, as I began to show almost immediately. Though nothing was ever said, I knew that the eyes on my belly in the market suspected that I had been pregnant before the wedding. So much gossip circulates in Nazareth anyway, and even the chance of such a scandal was too good for the people to pass up. Joseph shielded me from any potential embarrassment as much as he could. Often times he did the shopping and fetched water for us, things that normally only the women in town did, just to protect me. I wondered how he would do that when the time for the baby came. Turns out You had a plan in motion. The time for the birth approached, and the Roman government issued a decree for a census to be taken. I couldn't believe it. Nine months pregnant with Your child, and You wanted me to take to the road? The good part about the census was that I would not have to give birth under the suspicious eyes of the people of Nazareth. The hard part was the back of a donkey jostling me and my very full womb around on the rocky road into Bethlehem. My mom joked that it would be good for me, and would probably induce labor. Boy was she right. As if that wasn't enough, we had to settle for a stable versus a hotel room. Hardly the place I would choose for the Messiah to be born, and yet . . . well, You were there with me. I brought Your Son into the world in that tiny stable, laying out on a bed of hay. And now He sleeps in an animal trough converted into a makeshift cradle. In all the confusion and craziness, I nearly forgot exactly how all this began—with an angel and a promise. I was exhausted, tired, and wondered where You were in all this. Then came the shepherds, saying they too had seen angels. The angels told them the Messiah had been born, and when the shepherds saw my son—Your Son—they fell down and worshiped Him. And that was when it really hit me: as hard as these nine months have been, as intimidating as the gossip could get, I have never been more terrified than I am right now. I'm so young, Lord. And it's so soon for me to be having a family anyway. In so many ways, I'm still a child, and now, I'm responsible for another life. And not just any life, but the life of Your only Son! I've asked the question a hundred times and still can't find an answer. Why would You choose me? What qualities, what qualifications do I have that make me more remarkable than all the women in Israel? This is such a heavy burden to place on my shoulders, and yet You've done it, with absolute confidence and assurance. I think back time and time again to the angel. The warm look on his face. And the words he spoke, "For nothing is impossible with God." Does that really include making a child like me the woman to raise the Messiah? Who am I to teach Him the story of creation when He witnessed it? Who am I to teach Him the law of Moses when He was the one to author it? And will I be the one to tell Him of His destiny, that He will deliver Israel from oppression? How will I be able to discipline a child like Him? Or will that even be necessary? Will He be the one to chastise me and correct my actions when I sin? How will I explain to Him . . . how can I teach the immortal Son of God about death? So many questions. So few answers. But I guess for tonight, well, I don't have to know any of the answers, do I? Tonight He is a baby, so let Him rest. Let me rest as well. And please, please stay near me. I'm going to need all the strength and wisdom You can give me to fulfill the destiny You've given to me.

[Blackout.]

What Child Is This?

Handmade Christmas

by Diana R. Jenkins

Summary: SOPHIE hates MOM's idea that their family should make all their Christmas gifts this year. Who knows what kind of crummy presents her little brothers might make for her? Then her brothers' gifts turn out to be stranger than SOPHIE imagined—and amazingly meaningful!

Characters:

SOPHIE—the big sister to five little brothers

MOM—their mother, who has a different idea for Christmas

THEO—the oldest of SOPHIE's little brothers

KYLE—the next oldest brother

GABE and MIKE—the twins

JOEY—the youngest brother

Setting: *(by scene)*

Living room—a few chairs, Christmas tree

SOPHIE's bedroom—bed, table or desk, trash can

Boys' bedroom—table

Church—area to one side with cross on wall

Props: decorated Christmas tree; art supplies like crayons; tissue boxes; glitter; wrapping paper, etc.; gifts not wrapped: bookmarks; wrapped gifts: necklace; nightgown; colored rock; decorated tissue box that rattles; scroll; rainbow picture with penny on ragged piece of cardboard

Director's Notes: The little brothers can be played by young children but the play is more humorous if older actors perform these roles. The actors can wear oversized T-shirts, kids' cowboy hats, backwards baseball caps, and the like to add to the humor. The twins should each black out a tooth. Childlike mannerisms such as pouting, putting a finger to the lips, digging a toe into the rug, etc. can also help make these characters funny.

The entire cast is in the living room, frozen, as the play begins. They are just finishing up decorating their Christmas tree. SOPHIE walks forward to speak to the audience.

Sophie: I love Christmas! I mean *love* it! And I wanted this Christmas to be special since it was our first holiday without Dad. It's really hard when your parents break up, you know. Anyway, I wasn't too happy when Mom came up with her big idea about changing things. *[returns to place as everyone unfreezes]*

Mom: I think we should make our Christmas gifts this year instead of buying them!

Sophie: Are you joking?

Mom: Of course not! Just think—won't it be fun to think of an idea for each person?

Theo: Yeah!

Mom: And then figure out how to make the present?

Theo and Kyle: *[a little louder]* Yeah!

Mom: And then make the present out of stuff we have around here?

Theo, Kyle, Gabe and Mike: *Yeah!*

Mom: Just imagine how much fun it will be to see the person open the handmade gift!

[Boys cheer. Sophie sits with arms folded until the uproar dies down.]

Sophie: Are you joking?

Mom: Quit kidding around, Sophie. What do you really think?

Sophie: *[to audience as everyone freezes]* I knew Mom wanted me to like her idea. But what kind of terrible gifts would I get from my little brothers? I mean . . . they can't even color inside the lines! *[turns to Mom as everyone unfreezes]* I don't know, Mom.

Mom: Come on. A handmade Christmas will be fun!

Sophie: Yeah, you keep saying that, but . . .

Theo: Come on, Sophie!

Joey: Please, Sophie! Pleeeeeeeeeeeeeeeeeeeease!

All the Boys: Please! Please! Please!

Sophie: *[laughing]* Oh, all right, already!

Boys: *[cheer]* Yeah! That's right! Woohoo!

Mom: Thanks, Sophie.

Sophie: Sure. Whatever.

[MOM exits. The BOYS scramble off to their room, cluster around table, and work furiously on gifts during the next scene. Ever so often we glimpse crayons, a tissue box, wrapping paper, or some cardboard. Now and then a spurt of glitter or sequins bursts upwards.]

SOPHIE: *[to audience]* For the next week, the boys worked in secret on their gifts. They drove me nuts acting all mysterious about the whole thing.

KYLE: *[sticks head "out of room," sees SOPHIE]* Don't come in here!

SOPHIE: I'm not.

KYLE: Because the gifts are a secret.

SOPHIE: I know, Kyle!

KYLE: And very, very special! *[goes back to work]*

SOPHIE: *[to audience]* Like they could possibly be making anything good with old tissue boxes and glitter!

[MOM enters.]

SOPHIE: Mom, I just don't think this handmade Christmas is a good idea. I mean . . . who knows what they'll *[gesturing towards boys]* come up with.

MOM: That's the fun of it!

SOPHIE: Couldn't we just do things like we did when Dad was here? You know . . . one of you took the boys shopping and gave them money and helped them choose good gifts. That worked out great!

MOM: *[quietly]* I'm afraid we can't afford that this year. *[starts to exit]*

SOPHIE: Oh. Well, I'm sure the handmade thing will work out just fine. *[to audience]* Why didn't I think of that? I *knew* money had been tight since Dad left. I felt terrible about making Mom feel bad.

GABE: Hey, is there any more glitter?

THEO: Here's a whole jar!

SOPHIE: *[dreary]* But I still didn't want a handmade Christmas!

[Boys put gifts under Christmas tree and then exit, taking the table with them. SOPHIE watches, annoyed by their mysterious manner and then goes to her room.]

SOPHIE: *[to audience]* I was so depressed about Christmas being ruined that I didn't get around to making my gifts until Christmas Eve. Then I quickly made a necklace for Mom and some bookmarks for my brothers. *[takes gifts from table, shaking her head sadly]* This is going to be the worst Christmas ever!

[SOPHIE puts gifts under Christmas tree as MOM marches in, followed by boys in a line. They go to church area and SOPHIE joins them. Family mimes service, pretending to pray and sing, while SOPHIE talks to audience.]

SOPHIE: I guess the Christmas Eve service was lovely, but I just couldn't get into it. Dad wasn't with us. Mom looked sad. And I couldn't even look forward to opening gifts! After the service, I didn't want to go home and have that stupid handmade Christmas.

[Rest of family lines up, leaves church area, and gathers around Christmas tree.]

SOPHIE: *[sighs]* Might as well get it over with. *[joins family around Christmas tree]* Here, you guys. *[hands each boy a bookmark]*
GABE and MIKE: Wow! Bookmarks!
JOEY: Did you make these?
SOPHIE: Of course! *[glares at MOM]* Remember? We're having a handmade Christmas.
KYLE: You did a good job, Sophie.
SOPHIE: Uh . . . thanks. And here's something for you, Mom.
MOM: *[opens gift and pulls out necklace]* How pretty! Thank you, Sophie. *[hands gift to SOPHIE]* I made this for you.
SOPHIE: *[unwraps a nightgown]* Thanks, Mom. This is beautiful! *[everyone freezes as SOPHIE shows gift to audience]* My new nightgown was so great that I started thinking this handmade Christmas might be OK after all. *[returns to place as everyone unfreezes]*
JOEY: Here's my present for you, Sophie. *[hands her the gift]*
SOPHIE: Wow! It's as heavy as a rock! *[gets paper off, looks disappointed]* It *is* a rock. *[holds up a rock that's been colored with crayons]*

JOEY: I colored it myself.

SOPHIE: I can tell.

JOEY: Don't you just love it?

SOPHIE: Uh . . . yeah. Thanks, Joey.

GABE: Open our gift next!

MIKE: *[handing her a tissue box overly decorated with glitter, etc.]* Look inside.

SOPHIE: *[shakes box which makes something inside rattle]* Hmm, I wonder what it is. *[looks inside]* I see two little white things that . . . Ew! Are those teeth?

GABE and MIKE: *[pointing to missing teeth in mouths]* Yes!

SOPHIE: That is so dis . . . *[voice trails away as she notices MOM giving her a warning look]* fantastic. Yep, fantastic! Thanks, guys. *[sets box aside with a shiver of disgust]*

KYLE: *[hands SOPHIE a large scroll]* Open my present next, Sophie!

SOPHIE: *[unrolls scroll with KYLE's help. It's huge!]* You scribbled all over it, Herbert! *[looks down the whole length]* I mean *all* over it.

KYLE: I wrote it myself!

SOPHIE: No kidding. *[notices MOM frowning again]* I mean thanks! Good job!

THEO: *[handing SOPHIE his gift]* Here, Sophie. I hope you like it.

SOPHIE: *[takes out a ragged piece of cardboard, looks at it with great disappointment, speaks sarcastically]* Wow. A picture of a rainbow. On a hunk of cardboard. Wow.

THEO: Did you notice the penny?

SOPHIE: Oh, yeah. *[turns picture towards audience]* You glued down a penny for the pot of gold. Aw, Theo. This is just too much. *[MOM and boys gather up their gifts and exit as SOPHIE speaks to audience]* The nightgown Mom made me was really nice, but let's face it—one decent gift couldn't save this Christmas. I decided to go to bed and cry myself to sleep. *[carries gifts to bedroom, puts nightgown on over clothes]* Man! What a bunch of junk! *[tosses other gifts in trash can, goes to bed, sniffles for a bit and then falls asleep]*

BOYS: *[run into room]*

KYLE: Get up, Sophie!

THEO: It's time for breakfast!

GABE and MIKE: We're having pancakes!

JOEY: Hey, why is my rock in the trash?

SOPHIE: *[hides under the covers as BOYS dig things out of the trash can]*
THEO: What's this doing in here?
GABE: Here's our box!
MIKE: And our teeth!
KYLE: And my scroll!

[BOYS all turn and stare at the lump that's SOPHIE.]

SOPHIE: *[slowly peeks out]* I . . . uh . . . guess that stuff accidentally fell off my desk...or something . . . and uh . . . fell into the trash can. Heh. Heh.
JOEY: Oh, OK! *[petting the rock]* Don't you just love it? Creek rocks are so smooth.
SOPHIE: They sure . . . Hey, wait a minute. Is that the rock from our day at the park?
JOEY: Yep! That was fun!
SOPHIE: But you love that rock, Joey.
JOEY: *[handing rock to SOPHIE]* You can keep it.
SOPHIE: Thanks.
GABE: You forgot to put the teeth under your pillow . . .
MIKE: . . . and make a wish!
SOPHIE: Do you guys still believe that?
GABE: Sure!
MIKE: And we're giving you our wishes.
SOPHIE: Thanks! I'll do it tonight. *[notices KYLE holding scroll]* Kyle, does your scroll say something?
KYLE: I'll read it to you. *[loud,]* Sophie is the best sister in the world and she reads to me because she is the best sister in the world and she helps me with my shoelaces because she is the best sister in the world and she—
SOPHIE: Thanks, Kylet! I'll read the rest myself. Later, OK? *[sets scroll aside, then notices THEO with picture]* Theo, is there something special about your picture?
THEO: Sure! *[hands her the picture and points to penny]* That's Daddy's lucky penny at the end of the rainbow. He gave it to me before he left.

SOPHIE: *[Boys freeze and she looks at each face and then at the audience.]* I don't believe in lucky pennies, but right then I felt like the luckiest big sister in the world! I gave my brothers last-minute presents but their gifts really meant something! *[Boys unfreeze. SOPHIE hugs them.]* Thanks, guys! These are the best presents ever!

JOEY: *[claps and cheers]* Yeah! I knew you would like them!

SOPHIE: You don't have to cheer for me, Joey.

JOEY: I'm not! *[sniffs air]* I'm cheering for the pancakes!

MOM: *[from offstage]* Breakfast is ready!

[Blackout.]

A Shepherd's Voice
by Paula Reed

Summary: Sometime after the shepherds had visited the manger on the first Christmas Eve, one SHEPHERD returns to the field where he tells of the evening's event to his son, AARON, who has met him there. *[Related Scripture: Luke 2:8-20; Micah 5:4-5]*

Characters:

SHEPHERD—father of AARON, middle-aged man

AARON—son of the SHEPHERD, teen male

Props: backdrop to resemble a starry-night sky, artificial trees/plants, rocks for scenery

Costumes: Bible-times costumes

SHEPHERD appears pacing back and forth, obviously full of excitement and wonder over what he has just seen and heard.

SHEPHERD: I wonder if this night will be remembered? Will the generations to come understand the significance of this holy night?

[AARON runs in to join him, breathless and excited.]

AARON: Papa! I came as fast as I could when I heard the news!

SHEPHERD: *[embracing AARON when he runs in]* Aaron, my son, I am so glad to see you! I have much to tell you! And you must listen carefully to what I am about to say. Never forget this night and what it means to you, to our people. Nothing will be the same after tonight.

AARON: *[asking rapid fire questions]* But, father, is it true? Has the Messiah really come to save us? Is He strong? How did He get here? *[questions continue as father interrupts]*

SHEPHERD: *[Laughing at his son's excitement, he leads him to a rock.]* Sit here, my child, and let me start at the beginning. This has been no ordinary night, I tell you! I, along with your uncles and cousins, was tending the sheep. Night had fallen, but, oh, what a night. The stars seemed to sparkle and dance against the black, velvet sky. But for the bleating of the sheep, all was calm and quiet. Out in the open fields, the crisp, cool wind caused us to gather around the fire where we huddled for warmth. Your cousin, Nathaniel, had just joined us after his watch over the flock in the eastern field. I was just getting ready to leave and take his place when a light shone all around us— a light so radiant that we fell to the ground and covered our faces to escape it. We were terrified! It was as if Yahweh parted the sky like a curtain and poured Heaven's light down upon us.

AARON: *[excitedly]* Then what, father?

SHEPHERD: Then, my child, an angel appeared to us and he spoke.

AARON: A *real* angel? What did he say?

SHEPHERD: He was very real, Aaron. His garment was a brilliant white, his body glowing. His face was so kind, so gentle, and yet his voice rang across the fields commanding respect and attention. Even the sheep were silent! Trembling, we bowed our heads, but our fear soon turned to joy when he said, "Do not be afraid. I bring you good news of great joy that will be to you; for all the people. Today in the town of David a Savior has been born he is Christ the Lord. This will be a sign to you and you will find the baby wrapped in cloths lying in a manger." We turned to one another in amazement when suddenly there was an explosion of light and sound! The sky peeled open and a host of angels, mighty and glorious, joined with the angel singing and praising God. They sang, "Glory to God in the highest and on earth peace on whom his favor rests." Their voices filled the air with the sweetest, richest melody that man has ever heard. In complete awe and wonder, we lifted our faces and our hands, praising God with the angels. And then as quickly as they came, they left as the sky closed in around them. Our eyes had to adjust to the darkness once again, and we wondered aloud at what we had just witnessed.

AARON: So did you go, Papa—did you go see the baby?

SHEPHERD: We left the fields as fast as our feet could carry us and went into Bethlehem. And there, at the edge of the town, we found Him lying in a manger just as the angel said we would. We still couldn't believe that the Lord had brought this announcement to us, simple shepherds, but we knew we must be obedient and find the Christ child.

AARON: Tell me what you saw—what was it like?

SHEPHERD: When we first came to the stable, we were excited—all of us were talking at once about all that we had seen and heard. But something happened when we came to the manger and saw the babe wrapped in cloths and held by his young mother. Immediately a hush came over us and we were filled with a holy awareness. I have never felt anything like it before. We were hesitant at first, as we didn't want to intrude upon them or break the quietness of the moment. But the young mother, her name is Mary, and her husband, Joseph, beckoned us to come closer. And the closer we came to the Christ child the more we felt as if we were ushered into the very presence of the Lord Jehovah himself. We bowed in humble adoration, tears of joy streaming down our faces as our hearts accepted that we beheld our Messiah—the long awaited one! As I knelt before Him, His tiny, wrinkled hand, pushing through the hay and straw, touched mine, and I was filled with incredible peace.

AARON: I want to go to the stable too, Papa! But I still don't understand why He was born in a manger, instead of a palace.

SHEPHERD: I do not understand it myself, Aaron. I only know I saw and believed. Like most of our people, I had envisioned a mighty king and a vast army—someone who would conquer our oppressors with an iron hand. At the very least I imagined our Savior would be a rich and powerful ruler. I am only a simple shepherd, and we are the poorest of our people. And yet on this holy night, I feel as if I've been made rich because I've seen the Christ child. I dare not question Jehovah's plan for our salvation, and if it is found in the tenderness and gentleness of a baby, then so it shall be.

AARON: Did you take him a gift—a gift fit for a king?

SHEPHERD: I had nothing to offer Him but my faith and my trust. Somehow it seemed fit for our Redeemer—

AARON: [standing and tugging on his father] I can't wait to see Him, father! Will you take me now?

SHEPHERD: Yes, my son. And remember we must never forget this holy night. You must tell it to your children and your children's children. Come, let us go to the manger and worship our King!

[SHEPHERD and AARON exit. Blackout.]

No Room for Jesus

by Hamish Taylor

Summary: JESUS is auditioning for a part in the Thanksgiving play. He tries to convince the nonbelieving DIRECTOR that He has more to do with the holidays than just Easter and Christmas.
Cast:

DIRECTOR—male or female (TERRANCE or TRACY), rude, sarcastic, curt, and a little excitable

JESUS—middle-aged man, gentle, but persistent, calm

Setting: an audition room

Props: desk with various papers and stationary on it, phone, 2 scripts—one that the DIRECTOR has and a different one for JESUS

Director's note: There is an alternate section in the drama depending on whether the DIRECTOR is male or female.

Scene opens to the DIRECTOR sitting at the desk stage right, writing on some paper.

DIRECTOR: Next!

[JESUS enters from right.]

DIRECTOR: Name and part You're trying out for.

JESUS: I'm trying out for the part of Jesus.

DIRECTOR: *[looking through his script]* Ahhh, sorry, this is a Thanksgiving play. There's no Jesus part in it.

JESUS: I understand that, but I was thinking that perhaps there should be.

DIRECTOR: Well, sorry, no can do. No Jesus here. Next!

JESUS: I think that's a bit of a shame, don't you? There really ought to be something in the play about me.

DIRECTOR: About who? Look, buddy . . . *[sees JESUS for first time]* Whoa, nice hairdo. Anyway, if You want to play Jesus, we have an Easter pageant in April and a Christmas play in December—although, You may not fit in the manger, so I don't know. Other than that, You're out of luck. Now if You'll excuse me, I have a play to direct.

JESUS: I just don't think that Thanksgiving is really complete without me in it.

DIRECTOR: Look, Fabio, I already have a script right here. And guess what? No Jesus! I can't just rewrite the script so that any nut off the street can have a part. Understand?

JESUS: Well, actually, I have a script right here you can use.

DIRECTOR: *[sarcastically]* How did I know that was coming?

JESUS: You really ought to have a look at it.

DIRECTOR: So what, now You're a better scriptwriter than I am? All right, if I have a look at it, You have to promise to leave, OK? *[takes script and looks over it]* Look, it's a great script and all; it's just that . . . well . . . it doesn't really capture the essence of the season. I mean, really, this whole thing is about Jesus. Thanksgiving isn't about Jesus!

JESUS: Sure it is! It's all about me.

DIRECTOR: No, look. Thanksgiving is about getting off work, eating way too much turkey, and watching (your favorite NFL team) lose on TV. It has nothing to do with You. And what do You mean "You," anyway? Who do you think You are?

JESUS: You know exactly who I am.

DIRECTOR: OK, scary man. I think it's time that I pay a quick call to my good friends with those nice hug-yourself jackets.

JESUS: Look, Terrance *[or Tracy]*, you and I both know that I belong in this story.

DIRECTOR: How did You know my name? Do I need to call security?

JESUS: Hey, it's me! *[advances a step toward the DIRECTOR.]*

DIRECTOR: Whoa! Back off, weirdo! I know karate! *[DIRECTOR gets into the "crane" position—standing on one leg, with arms up in the air and hands pointing forward]* No one can defeat the crane!

JESUS: Terrance, stop, please. You're embarrassing yourself. We both know you got all your moves from the *Karate Kid* movies. Now I just want people to see the role that I play in Thanksgiving. I really think people are missing out on the true meaning of the holiday.

DIRECTOR: OK, Jesus, or whoever You are, now You're starting to get on my nerves. What's Your big deal about taking over all of the holidays? It's bad enough that You have a monopoly on Christmas and Easter. Can't You just leave Thanksgiving to us?

JESUS: Who do you think you're giving thanks to, anyway?

No Room for Jesus

DIRECTOR: *[pauses]* Butterball®?

JESUS: No, Terrance (or TRACY), listen to me. You are giving thanks to God for all the wonderful blessings He has given to you. You know— creation, food, shelter, and all that stuff. Haven't you seen the Bible?

DIRECTOR: I was in court once . . .

JESUS: Yeah, I remember that. You probably shouldn't do that again. Anyway, if you would *read* the Bible, you would see that the biggest reason you should be thankful is the sacrifice that I made for your sins. See, this holiday really *is* about me.

DIRECTOR: *[awkward pause]* Well, OK, thank You Mr. Man. I appreciate You coming by, but we don't have anything for You right now. Try again in April. Next!

JESUS: I'm sorry you feel that way. You can't find any way to include me?

DIRECTOR: Sorry. Nothin' doin'. You've got Your two choices: Christmas and Easter. Take it or leave it. We'll call You if we ever do a play on the second coming. Other than that, You're outta luck. There's simply no room in Thanksgiving for Jesus.

JESUS: I can see that. *[leaves]*

DIRECTOR: *[shaken up a bit]* Next!

[Blackout.]

How Thankful You Must Be

by Carol S. Redd

Summary: A Thanksgiving reminder that sometimes we take for granted the things for which we should be most thankful.

Characters:

SUSAN—middle-aged woman, overcommitted, exhausted, and in need of a favor

VALERIE—middle-aged woman, overcommitted, exhausted, and in need of a favor

RUTH—middle-aged woman, overcommitted, exhausted, and in need of a favor

LISA—middle-aged woman, overcommitted, exhausted, and in need of a favor

FAYE—middle-aged woman, overcommitted, exhausted, and in need of a favor

Setting: large screen *(for* PowerPoint® *slides)* in clear view of audience

Props: projector set up for Power Point®, 8 PowerPoint® slides with the following statements:

1. If you are *that* thankful each time someone takes your place . . .
2. . . . baking a cake
3. . . . coaching a team
4. . . . teaching a Sunday school class or
5. . . . cleaning a house
6. How thankful you must be when you remember . . .
7. I took your place.
8. *[picture or silhouette of Jesus on cross]*

Costumes: modern-day clothing

As drama begins, SUSAN is facing right, followed by VALERIE, RUTH, LISA, and FAYE. All five characters are facing right and standing directly behind one another across the width of the stage [in order as stated]. Characters are spaced approximately one foot apart [audience is viewing the left profile of all characters]. SUSAN turns to VALERIE who is standing directly behind her.

SUSAN: Hi, Valerie! How are you?

VALERIE: I'm pretty good . . . and you?

SUSAN: Well, to be perfectly honest, I just remembered I promised to bake a cake for a dinner at church tomorrow afternoon and I've been so busy, I totally forgot about it. And I've got another commitment tonight that I just can't get out of. I don't even have time to run to the store and buy ingredients. It just has to be something homemade . . . I gave my word.

VALERIE: Don't be so upset about it . . . I'll do it for you.

SUSAN: What?

VALERIE: I'll go home and make a homemade cake for you and take it to church with me in the morning.

SUSAN: I could *never* ask you to do that . . .

VALERIE: No, really, I will . . . I don't mind at all. Matter of fact, I would be more than happy to help you out.

SUSAN: *[extremely excited]* Oh my! You are so great! I can't believe you would do that for me . . . thank you so very much! I owe you a favor . . . a BIG favor.

[VALERIE turns to RUTH who is standing directly behind her.]

VALERIE: Hi Ruth! How are you?

RUTH: I'm pretty good . . . and you?

VALERIE: Well, to be perfectly honest, I've kind of gotten myself in a bind. I've been coaching my daughter's basketball team and this Saturday, is their big game. If they win this Saturday they'll get to play in the tournament. But I just found out I have to work this weekend. I don't know how to tell the team. I mean, I'm their only coach. My assistant moved at the end of last year, and I haven't been able to find anyone to help me. We've got practice scheduled tonight. I guess I'll just have to tell them there's not going to be a Saturday game after all.

RUTH: Well, what about me?

VALERIE: What do you mean?

RUTH: Well, I used to play basketball and even coached one season a few years ago. Maybe I could help you out.

VALERIE: You would do that for me?

RUTH: Sure . . . I'd be happy to. Just let me know what time tonight's practice is, and I'll be there so I can get to know the players . . . and they can get to know me.

VALERIE: *[extremely excited]* I can't believe you! I still hate that I'll miss the game . . . but not having to let the team down . . . wow! What can I say? You're the best!

[RUTH turns to LISA who is standing directly behind her.]

RUTH: Hi, Lisa! How are you?

LISA: I'm pretty good . . . and you?

RUTH: Well, to be perfectly honest, I'm not doing very well right now. I just found out that some of my friends are going out of town Sunday for a few days. I *really* want to go with them but this is the Sunday I volunteered to teach a Sunday school class. I can't believe everything always hits at the same time! I mean, it's not that I don't want to teach . . . but I don't get to see much of my friends anymore. I just wish there was a way I could do both!

LISA: Why don't you let me help you out?

RUTH: What do you mean? How could you help?

LISA: Why don't you let me take your turn teaching Sunday school?

RUTH: You're kidding! You would do that for me?

LISA: Sure, I'm probably not as good of a teacher as you are, but I'd be glad to take your place.

RUTH: *[extremely excited]* I can't believe you! I don't know what to say . . . but thanks! Thank you SO much!

[LISA turns to FAYE who is standing directly behind her.]

LISA: Hi, Faye! How are you?

FAYE: I'm pretty good . . . and you?

LISA: Well, to be perfectly honest, my in-laws are coming to stay with us for the weekend, and my house is an absolute mess. I was sick the first part of the week and now that I'm back to work, I'm exhausted. The last thing in the world I feel like doing is cleaning the house.

FAYE: What if I help you?

LISA: Help me? How?

FAYE: Let me come over and clean your house for you.

How Thankful You Must Be

LISA: There's no way I could let you do that!

FAYE: I'm serious. I used to work for a cleaning service, and I love to clean . . . really. I don't have anything special planned for tomorrow, so while you're at work, just let me come over and clean. I'll have it done in five hours tops.

LISA: *[extremely excited]* You are incredible! I can't believe you would do that for me!

[ALL freeze in place—lights go out—slides slowly and silently presented on screen. Blackout.]

No Turkey in the Terminal

by John Cosper

Summary: Three friends stranded at the airport find plenty to be thankful for on Thanksgiving Day.

Characters:

ANNOUNCER—intercom announcer at an airport

SHARON—woman in 20s or 30s, wearing a Detroit Lions shirt, disgruntled about being stranded at the airport

GEORGE—man in 20s or 30s

BRIAN—man in 20s or 30s

Setting: airport terminal on Thanksgiving, table and chairs

Props: duffel bags, suitcases, table and chairs, a box of Chinese food (including egg rolls), soft drinks, bag from a giftshop, junk food, soda, a John Grisham novel

Costumes: modern-day clothes, Detroit Lions shirt for SHARON

ANNOUNCER: May I have your attention please. Delta Air Lines wishes to report all flights for the day are canceled due to inclement weather. All Delta customers please report to the service counter so that we can arrange other transportation or lodging. Thank you.

Lights up. SHARON sits at a table in an airport, her head on the table in exhaustion and frustration. Duffel bags and suitcases are stacked up beside her.

SHARON: All I wanted was a little time off. A fun vacation with my best friends before the holidays. And what do I get? Two days of being stranded in an airport, a thousand miles from home.

[GEORGE enters carrying a bag from the gift shop.]

SHARON: Tell me you got something. Tell me we're having Thanksgiving dinner!

GEORGE: Oh yeah, it's dinnertime!

SHARON: Great! I am so hungry. Did you find some turkey?

GEORGE: No.

SHARON: Pumpkin pie?

GEORGE: No.

SHARON: Cranberries?

GEORGE: No.

SHARON: Sweet potatoes, stuffing?

GEORGE: Uh, no.

SHARON: *[sniffs sadly]* Green bean casserole?

GEORGE: Ick, no!

SHARON: Then what do you have?

GEORGE: *[emptying the contents of the bag onto the table]* A feast for a king, Sharon. We've got . . . soda, beef jerky, nachos, chips, hard candy, chewy candy, chocolate candy, snack cakes, and . . . the latest best seller from John Grisham! That's for me.

SHARON: George, you were supposed to get Thanksgiving dinner!

GEORGE: It's Thanksgiving. It's lunchtime. Chow down.

SHARON: This is *not* Thanksgiving dinner, George! This is a computer nerd's breakfast.

GEORGE: Sharon, we're snowed in. The grocery stores are closed. This is the best I could do.

SHARON: Well it stinks.

GEORGE: Suit yourself. More for me!

SHARON: Go ahead! Gorge yourself on imitation Thanksgiving. I hope Brian does a little better, because I'm starving.

GEORGE: Mmmm, nothing like a bag of chips when you're starving.

SHARON: Nothing but Thanksgiving dinner!

[BRIAN enters with a box of carryout Chinese food and a soda.]

BRIAN: Hey, guys. Oooh, Slim Jims! Nice.

SHARON: Brian, please tell me you found some real food.

BRIAN: Fear not, my lady. I brought us all a complete Thanksgiving meal.

SHARON: You got it? Turkey, cranberries, pumpkin pie?

BRIAN: No, not exactly.

SHARON: Then what?

BRIAN: I brought dinner from the Chinese place in terminal B!

GEORGE: You're kidding!

BRIAN: Nope. Ladies and gents, I give you Brian's Thanksgiving feast!

[BRIAN opens the box.]

SHARON: Fried rice? Beef and broccoli? Egg rolls?

BRIAN: And three fortune cookies!

SHARON: I don't believe it. Chinese food for Thanksgiving!

GEORGE: I know, it's a holiday miracle!

SHARON: It's awful!

BRIAN: What's wrong?

SHARON: What isn't wrong, Brian? Thanksgiving is Thanksgiving for four reasons. Turkey, cranberries, pumpkin pie, and football!

BRIAN: Is that what makes Thanksgiving? I always wondered about that.

GEORGE: At my house it's Grandma telling my mom everything she's doing wrong in the kitchen, while Grandpa tells all of us grandkids how soft and weak we are.

BRIAN: Yeah, and at my house, before we carve the turkey, Dad goes around the table to tell each of us how we disappointed him that year.

SHARON: Sorry about your luck. Back home, right about now, my family is finishing off the first round of feast and preparing to watch the Detroit game. And what do we have here? Canceled flights, beef jerky, and egg rolls! This is a disaster.

GEORGE: Sharon, I know it stinks that we won't be home for Thanksgiving, but I think you're missing the point of the holiday.

SHARON: No, George, I don't think I am.

GEORGE: Sharon, it's Thanksgiving. Not Turkey Day, not Pumpkin Pie Day, but Thanksgiving. It's a day to remember the good things we have and be thankful.

SHARON: Thankful? This is the one time a year all my sisters are home, and you expect me to be thankful?

GEORGE: I know you're missing time with your sisters, but even here, we have plenty to be thankful for.

BRIAN: He's right, Sharon. We're stranded hundreds of miles from home, but at least we're not alone. I'm with my two best friends. I'm having a great time. And I have egg rolls.

GEORGE: Yeah. We had a great vacation. We're all healthy. No one got sick.

SHARON: That's true. Brian didn't barf once on the way here. And he always gets sick on planes.

No Turkey in the Terminal

BRIAN: And aren't you glad I didn't? If I had lost it, you might not have met that hot guy on the flight here.

SHARON: Yeah, Kevin was pretty sweet.

GEORGE: And you got his number.

SHARON: Oh, knock it off, you guys. I was having a perfectly good sulk before you had to go Linus on me.

BRIAN: Sorry, Sharon. But I'm having a good time being here with you all. God's been too good for me to get all upset over a little turkey.

GEORGE: Me too.

SHARON: Yeah, me three.

GEORGE: You know, Sharon, I think I saw some deli sandwiches at the gift shop that had turkey. I can go check for you if you want.

SHARON: No, that's OK. [snatches an egg roll] Once I get the smell of an egg roll in my nostrils, nothing else satisfies.

BRIAN: Help yourself. I'll get more.

SHARON: I guess this is a pretty decent Thanksgiving after all. I thank God for you clowns every day, but how often do we take the time to sit and really share or appreciate each other?

GEORGE: Not often.

SHARON: Maybe that's why we're here. I love you guys, and I want you to know—

ANNOUNCER: Your attention please. US Airways is announcing all our flights for the day are now canceled. However, all stranded passengers are welcome to watch the Lions game now playing on the large screen TV in our US Airways Club Lounge in terminal C.

[SHARON, BRIAN, and GEORGE get up, grabbing their food and luggage.]

SHARON: We'll resume the love fest after the game!

BRIAN: Amen to that!!

[Blackout.]